KUNDALINI RISING

Songs of Power and Spirit

by
Honora Finkelstein

El Amarna Publishing

EL AMARNA PUBLISHING

ISBN-13: 978-0615666006
ISBN-10: 0615666000

Printed in the United States of America

El Amarna Publishing
Grayville, IL
Visit our website at www.ElAmarnaPublishing.com

Dedication

To Susan, who helps me grow—
"The beautiful woman has come."

KUNDALINI RISING

Songs of Power and Spirit

Contents

Deja Vu

They (the arbiters of taste and art and literature,
Bestowers of the benison of fame)
They say, "One cannot be a poet
Unless he has a certain sense of place—
A knowledge of his 'roots,'
An understanding of the heritage from which he's sprung!"
And they delight in affectatious dialect—
A drawl or twang or brogue to demonstrate they have been graced
With sufficient overlay of place
To bear the title "poet."

"But what," I ask, in my quietest, most self-effacing manner,
"What of the certain sense of *self*?
Does that not give *me* the right to write?"

For the "sense of place" is sometimes—often—more than I can bear—
I have been many places, and I find that everywhere
I go, I know, yes, *know* that I have been before.
Each new hamlet a homecoming to my self—
Sometimes bountiful...
Sometimes painful...

Beneath the wheels of the carriage,
I watched my sweet husband die—
His blood on the wet cobblestones not red—
Becoming dirty pinkish gray in the Paris gutter,
Transmuted by the rain...

Chanting the Latin words,
I knelt and scoured the worn, grey stones,
Murmuring prayers at Evensong—
Et benedictus fructus ventris tui Jesus—
Quietly yearning for the joy
Of some sweet woman's smile...

An ancient squaw
With withered breasts and wrinkled parchment face,
I yearned for the pleasure of not being owned
By my husband's whim.
Haggard and venerable,
I practiced and learned to love
Sweet discipline...

Trim, muscular, the image in the mirror says,
"I am the Fencing Master of all France;
The Dauphin's in my charge—
My Wheel of Fortune risen to its zenith"...

I died in prison, naked, whipped, and bleeding,
Thighs pinioned wide,
For all the churlish guards
To take their pleasure...

I died in bed—
The woman under me was not my wife,
But a harlot who'd agreed to let me take my ease
For two loaves of my best bread...

Demure maiden, face-whited with rice powder...

Brave general, envy of his troops,
Devourer of the Hittites...

And so it goes.
My Self weighs heavy on me.

To the arbiters of art and fame, I say:
Each place I go, I feel with certainty
The intimations of my immortality.

And for sweet Keats' sake...
Whatever happened to
Negative capability?

Alien Laughter

"Where I come from," the visitor said,
   "we laugh more than you do.
"It makes a mighty wind, and shakes the crystal trees
   to their foundations."

"Laugh for me," I coaxed, always testing.

And when he did, I clearly saw inside my head
   the crystal trees he spoke of
   shed their stained glass leaves,
   and swirling purple winds
   lift clouds of sparkling dust
   at the excitement.

And yet it was a joyous torrent,
   a sound so full of light and roaring pleasure
   that it hurt,

For I had never heard that sound before,
   and might not hear its like again on Earth.

"Where are you from?" I asked
   when his reverberations died away.

"From Jupiter," he said, with the tiniest of smiles.
"We're known all over the galaxy for our laughter."

Honora Finkelstein

On Finding the Beloved

Once there was a Sufi teacher
who was revered by his students
because he knew all there was to know
  from books.

He knew all about God and the heavens and the angels
  theoretically.

But he had never been set afire by God
  personally.

One day a mad Dervish climbed over the wall of the house
where the Sufi teacher was instructing his students;
the Dervish ran to the teacher, scooped up his books,
and threw them into the fountain in the courtyard, saying,
  "Now you must learn to live what you know."

The teacher, dismayed at having soggy books, jumped up to rescue them.
But as he did so, he looked into the eyes of the Dervish...
and for the first time fell into love with the divine spirit within.

Thus enrapt at last, he became like a holy madman,
following the Dervish everywhere,
singing songs of joy in acknowledgement
that God exists simultaneously in the act of loving,
and that finding the divine Beloved in another human form
can mirror and magnify the divine in oneself.
How sweet to love! How joyous! How transcendent!

And so at last he became a true teacher,
  for he had been set afire,
  had finally learned to live what he knew,
  and had encountered God in the process.

I was like the Sufi teacher,
   full of knowledge,
  but lacking the real knowing of passionate living
   until I looked into your eyes and saw the divine Beloved.

You have taught me more than you can ever know.
Thank you for throwing my books in the water.

Risks

The child has made me vulnerable.

Tottering like a tiny rubber-legged clown,
The steps he takes bring falls and sometimes
    tears from him and always
    fears from me.

For my sake I would cushion his advances,
Gather him up and rock him close a day or two yet.

Instead, I laugh and call him "brave" or "daring,"
    the better to prepare us for the price
    we both must pay for his growing up.

Honora Finkelstein

For John Rechy

I'd read each of your books a dozen times.
I'd been inside your soul for months
And anguished for the life you choose to lead,
The murky nightstalk,
Pausing on the corner of each street,
Or in the smoky bars or allnight theaters
Where you do not go to drink or watch
But look instead for johns who'll come on with you
And pay to offer you the adoration,
The thrill, the love you cannot live without.
I'd prayed for peace for you,
And blessed you cross the miles and living styles
That lay between us.
And time and time again, I questioned why
You'd chosen so much self-inflicted pain.

And then one afternoon,
I dozed over my work
And crossed the barrier of time
To a village in New England,
And saw you, dour and pinched of countenance
And dressed in black,
To mourn the death of purity.
With ugly leather whip
You flogged the gentle youngman to the ground
For lying with his brother.
Each time he tried to rise
You beat him back;
The blood ran down his face into his eyes.
You tore the collar from the wretched woman's dress,
And when she knelt before you,
Quivering in her shame,
You burned her breasts and back
With hot iron brands.

You never slacked your vigilant surveillance—
You weren't afraid to cast the crucial stone
That stirred the mob to action.
And so it was you came to bear the name,
"The Scourge of Salem."

Dear gentle John, who lives with daily torment,
Compulsion driven to play a self-defeating numbers game
In darkened parks and alleys and latrines.
So sure you're cursed of God you must deny that God exists.

For scouring homosexuals and whores
From out your village,
You've chosen to reverse and play their roles,
To pay out all at once the heavy debt
You built that somewhen long ago
In a town whose name's synonymous with "peace."

Honora Finkelstein

Homo Sum

With yellow strain around his eyes,
The young man turned to me and cried,
"My friend tried suicide!
He said he's do it, but I didn't buy it.
I laughed and went out for a coke and fries.
While I was out, he took a bunch of pills
        that I'd left on the shelf.
Oh, God, I couldn't call the cops;
I took him to the hospital myself!"

He sat to weep
And I sat down by him
And gently held his shoulder and his hand.
"How is he now?" I asked.
He crumpled, letting tears fall on my jacket,
And sobbed, "The worst part was,
I had to wait 'til he lost consciousness,
Or he'd have fought me when I tried to move him.
I'd never tried to pick him up before,
And he was heavy, and I had to drag him.
We aren't gay, and so I'd never touched him,
        except to shake his hand.
He was so…heavy."

I stroked his hair, and rocked him in my arms,
And touched his forehead lightly with my lips,
And wished protection for him from more harm.

"We aren't gay."
The words hung there,
Victims of a vigilante culture.

My throat constricted and my eyes filled, too;
I held him tightly as he sat and cried.
I wondered just how long a time he'd spend
Before he'd come to terms with why his friend
Had tried the suicide.

Signs and Portents

Disembarking from the plane,
I saw the sign, *"Wilkommen heim."*

It was an omen.

Three days we shared our vision, laughter, magic—
Visited places we'd not viewed before, of inner and outer worlds.
Our former wisdom quantum factoring,
We saw the ribbons of our hearts entwine,
In ancient Scandinavian design,
Never to be unwoven.

After our precious morning spent together, you hugged me close and
    whispered, "Welcome home."

I am so glad I found myself in you.

Honora Finkelstein

Somerset Encounter

She's not the only ghost on the plantation.
Charlotte, I mean, the free Black on the third floor.

Some places on the grounds are heavy with the presences
       of those who birthed and lived and worked and died here.

The crumbled piles of bricks that mark the hospital
       have residue of agony energy.
And Lovey's rape by the soldier in the kitchen
       sometimes replays to make the sensitive uncomfortable enough
       to skip lunch,
       without knowing why.

Still, the overlay of life force
       is generally light:
              Sukey's children playing,
              and the simple earthy cycles of days and seasons—
              of working, cooking, eating, reproducing,
              just celebrating life—
These are the things imprinted on this space.

The consciousness of being free or slave
       was not in every moment.
              Only some.

Life more important than the "way of life"
       is what lives on.

Sort of Sonnet

Across the stretch of grainy, sun-cracked asphalt,
Zigging from a yard to yonder sand lot,
And turning purple-brown from head to hind,
A lizard—frightened by one of my kind.
Not knowing now what color to become,
He stopped his change, his tail a tender azure,
Then scooted back across the sticky tar-top
To hide confusion in my neighbor's lawn.
Blest creature, in a moment you'll be mended,
Unlike the Homosapiens who stunned you,
The "thinking man" whose motley mental constructs
So often wear the skin of faulty judgment,
But who must live with injudicious error
Because he walks an all-too-public pavement.

Sometimes

sometimes, unexpectedly
a bar of music
or the scent of potpourri
or other synesthetic memory
will bring your face before me

and I'll stop
and smile
and gently touch
the corners of your mouth again
with tender fingers

it was never meant to be
more than it was
but while it was, it was
enough

Treehouse Refrain

Come to the treehouse, my dearest, my darling,
Come to the treehouse down in the glen—
We'll sit knee to knee high up in the tree
And sing each other sweet love songs again.

Come to the treehouse, my beloved, my beauty,
Come to the treehouse down in the glen—
We'll kneel face to face in tender embrace,
And I'll get to kiss your lips once again.

Come to the treehouse, my sweetheart, my sister,
Come to the treehouse down in the glen—
For you are my mirror, and when we're together
I know I'll feel myself whole once again.

Honora Finkelstein

Song of Remembrance

Last night I dreamed a far past memory:

The desert nights were warm
As we lay in the silken tent of our master.
We touched with sweetness
        And the tenderness of roes, nuzzling their young.
And we were young and fair of face and flesh.

Remember with me—
        The desert nights were warm,
        The stars were soft and bright,
        And you and I were one,
        O, my sister.
Do you remember?

Our master learned of our tenderness and touching
And sold me to an infidel chief.
Do you remember, my beloved?

My nights were dry and bitter,
And filled with the pain of forced taking.
And the desert winds blew hot and burned
        my face and flesh.
And I was with child by the infidel chief.

Where are you, my beloved?
In silence, with a muted tongue and voice,
I cried your name each moment of each night,
And my heart came apart beneath my breasts.

And when my time came to deliver the infidel's burden
        from my body,
I went into the desert by myself,
And dug a pit in the blistering sands,
Crawled into it and clenched my thighs until
        the child died,
        and I with it.

Where have you been these centuries,
        my sister, my soul, my beloved?

Let me kiss you with the kisses of my mouth,
For your touch is like a fountain in the desert.

R. I. P.

Here lie the remains of Homer L. Mensch, Ph.D.,
Who died in a session of Freshman English 103,
Taken off by adrenal-related apoplexy,
When he learned out of thirty students only two or three
Had read their assigned Herman Melville short story.

Before he expired he was heard to murmur softly,
"O Lord, what ridiculous fools these freshmen be!"

The English Department staff
Has chosen the following epitaph
To appear on Mensch's stone at the cemetery:

"Cast ye not pearls before sleepy swine, lest they snore loudly at thee!"

Honora Finkelstein

The Phantom Lover

It happened at a time
When I desired to be possessed,
A victim of the Venus Fly-Trap Syndrome.
After our first night together,
You sent two dozen roses,
With a card that said my skin was like
The softness of the petals.

I couldn't understand, quite, why you needed me.
Other men had, of course,
But they had known my nature first—
My compulsion to be compassionate and helpful—
While you I had seen only twice in company of friends.
Alone, you caught me in the hall,
And kissed me with an urgency
I'd not expected in a man
So settled and so seemingly secure.

For those three weeks, I dressed in lace,
Because you asked me to.
Sipped brandy on your balcony—
Absorbed the evening's fragrance from Jackson Square
        above the *Vieux Carre*—
Took walks with you in St. Louis Cemetery.

I thought you such a gentleman—
You never pressed me to make love the way that others had.
I must admit you would have been successful.
You said that twice you'd tried to die, and that I gave you
        something sweet to live for.
You also said that when we'd wed
You would express your passion in delicious, wicked ways.
And so, because you seemed so sure,
I took the ring you offered,
Desperate to keep the pleasure of your lips and arms and eyes.

But you weren't real.

The stories you had told me of your background and your life
I found weren't true.
And when I asked you why you'd had to lie,
You didn't even answer.
You simply raised an eyebrow, stood,
And walked from the cafe.

I tried to phone, but you were never in,
        or so your butler said.
And for two silent years, I lived with subtle questions.

Last week I saw you walking in the Quarter,
Your arm around another tender lover—
You looked into his eyes adoringly.

And then at last I understood
Why you had needed me.

Honora Finkelstein

Sweet Are the Uses

I'm not a masochist
But I sometimes welcome pain
To terminate relationships
Or mitigate the strain
Of holding in annoyances
Until I go insane.

I sometimes welcome pain.

Roses of Sharon

I

I have breathed the breath of life and felt the quickening
    of what must be my divinity.

Daily I grow stronger and richer
    with the mindless peace of creation.

Place your hand on my belly
    and know,
    if you can,
    what, where, and how God is.

Do not try to reason,
    but pause and listen,
And you may hear me singing
    Mary's song.

II

In the middle of the warm white fog of the hospital bed,
    I had a funny thought, to wit:

The contracting of a womb in labor
    as a new life presses forth
Is very like the spasming and jerking
    of the organs which initially seeded that life.
Pain may be directly proportional to pleasure,
    as Newton's law becomes a word made flesh.

When you come to such an ending,
Breathe,
    hold,
        push,
            remember
the beginning,
Smile as you bite down on your knuckle,
    And be a woman.

19

Limited Warranty

"What shall I do in human form?"
    said the man who would be king.

"If I go into a woman's womb,
    I must come out again.

"To be born in pain and to die in pain
    is the circular lot of men.

"If I go into human form,
    what will become of *me?*"

There's never any guarantee,
    said a little voice in his brain.

Success and failure are the same,
    But there's never permanent harm.

We may win the heights where the angels sing,
    or finish our days in gloom.

We choose our paths for the sake of growth,
    but they all end at the tomb.

If you really want to know the truth,
    life's quite a remarkable game,
    God/Goddess playing a song with Self,
    and you'll play it or sing it again and again,
    and again, and again, and again.

A Parable of the Cave

We each of us live in a cave of rock-hard walls,
That we erect to defend ourselves
From perceived attacks from others.

I perceived an attack from you,
          my brother,
And crawled into my cave to lick my wounds,
And sit alone in the darkness.

But I missed the dawn
          inside my cave
So I gathered my strength
          and came back out.

It's so much warmer living in the light.

Last night I heard you cry out in your sleep
In the darkness of your cave.
And I heard and felt your pain.

I call you, little brother.
Come out and take my hand.
Let us sit in the warm light together.

Honora Finkelstein

No Dwarves, No Princes

Once on a time, a princess slept sound
In a lovely coffin in the woods.
She had no PR agent, no dwarves to guard her,
And no princes knew she was there.

One day, a princess whose job is was
To wake other princesses rode through the wood.
She saw the coffin, climbed down from her horse,
And gave the princess a kiss.

The sleeping princess woke and said,
"Oh, thank you for waking me! Tell me, please,
Since I'm new at having this kind of relationship,
What do we do now?"

The princess whose job it was to wake princesses
Looked at the wide-awake princess in shock.
She took a step back, and mounting her horse, said,
"What do you mean *we*?"

"Well, um, I mean, uh, aren't we
Supposed to be going off together?
Maybe to an enchanted castle?
That's what the fairy tales say."

"My job description only includes
A wake-up call," said the other princess.
Besides, I have my own princess at home."
And she and her horse rode away.

So the wide awake princess climbed out of the coffin
And wandered off to reason why
She'd had to wake up from a comfortable sleep.
The answer is existential:

Living happily ever after
Is a personal choice each princess must make.
So take your power and seize the day.
You'll succeed if you just stay awake!

Millie's Party

We're sorry we missed Millie's party.
It must have been quite a soiree.
The people who showed up were charming,
Delightful, exciting, and gay.

We're sorry we missed Millie's party.
The food was the best in the town.
There was wine, there was beer, and a lot of good cheer.
People boogied and really got down.

We're sorry we missed Millie's party.
All the funniest people were there.
And two of the folks told the naughtiest jokes,
So the rest of them let down their hair.

We're sorry we missed Millie's party.
The dancing went on all night long.
The music excited, and passions ignited
When Millie took off her sarong.

We're sorry we missed Millie's party.
All the party animals came,
And they had so much fun to the very last one
That nobody was ever the same.

We're sorry we missed Millie's party,
For even up to this day,
When her guests shop for groceries they tarry
And pick up new friends on the way.

We're sorry we missed Millie's party,
But we didn't know Millie back then.
And we don't know her yet,
But we do hope we get
To meet her before
She throws a great party again.

(This poem was written with Susan Smily after we were told by a new friend we met at a grocery store that we looked familiar, and she asked if she'd met us at Millie's party. Sadly, since we were from out of town, we didn't know Millie, so we had missed the party. It's now 12 years later, and unfortunately, we still don't know Millie!)

Honora Finkelstein

Speculation

What would the preachers do if the devil was saved?
What would the preachers do if HE weren't so depraved?
What if he turned in his pitchfork,
And said, "I'm sorry I misbehaved!"?
What would the preachers do if the devil was saved?

What would the preachers do if the devil went straight?
Could they stay in bed on Sundays and sleep late?
Or would they still need to talk at us
About that old strait gate?
What would the preachers do if the devil went straight?

And what would the rest of us do if the devil turned good,
If he started preaching love and brotherhood?
Would we hang our heads in shame
'Cause we'd have nobody left to blame?
What would the rest of us do if the devil turned good?

Homage to Brit Lit

For Beowulf and Grendel,
For Macbeth and all his capers,
For Samuel Johnson and his rock,
And Mr. Pickwick's papers,

For Chaucer and his pilgrimage
    to the church at Canterbury,
For Peter Pan and Neverland
    from the mind of James M. Barrie,

For Alice's rabbit, and Thackeray's Fair,
For Lamb's pig dissertation,
For "Gunga Din," *The Invisible Man*,
    and Bunyan's destination,

For Churchill's work on war's Dunkirk,
For Wordsworth's sister dear,
For Marlowe, and Bacon, and Donne, and such,
For G&S songs that cheer,

For Elizabeth Barrett of Wimpole Street
    and the Browning with whom she was smitten—
For the spectrum of English lit we enjoy,
    We pay our tribute to Britain.

Descent of the Phoenix

Blessed be the names of the Lord
For it is said the world will never end
'Til all His names are spoken.

The masses do not heed me
When I speak of the sacred nature of mankind.
Perhaps it is because I am a woman
(One does not expect the Christ to be a woman).
Nevertheless, there are moments when I, even I,
Am vouchsafed the grace to speak the truth.

(Say the secret word tonight, and the phoenix will fly down and give you a kiss
on the forehead.)

Forego your guilt, there is no longer need.
For I, who am a woman,
Forgive you your transgressions.

I have invoked the visions of the Universal Mind,
And learned they are the same for each of us.
My joy news is a knowledge that for each the phoenix waits,
Ready to come to holy life at the sound of the sacred word.
And it's in this language of the soul
We can recognize our oneness—
Subconscious unity in variety.

Not scientific proof, you say?
No matter.
(Indeed, not matter at all, but only energy,
The complex web of light touching light,
And I have seen it in the core of each of you,

And pulsating among you,
Each touching other.)

Peel away the layers of the mind,
Like the skins of a pearl onion,
And you'll find
That mind at base is universe.

Hail, Lucifer, bearer of the Light,
Who led us to the knowledge of our recurrent night.
(Without the dark,
what perspective would one have upon the day?)

Hail, Joshua ben Joseph, who has come, time and again,
To lead us from the bondage of the guilt we label sin.
(Resurrection, transmutation into energy—
Intuition's knowledge that the *I* becomes one with *Infinity*.)

What is the secret word?
Tell me *your* name.
I promise, if you tell me, I will bless it.

About the Author

Honora Finkelstein has been an intelligence officer with the U.S. Navy, a small-press publisher, a technical writer, and a prize-winning features editor for Arundel Communications in Northern Virginia. She has been widely published in newspapers, magazines, and journals, has co-authored two nonfiction books, and has taught futurist and self-development workshops across the United States, in Canada, and in Europe. In the 1990s she produced and hosted a talk show on self-development and futurist topics called *Kaleidoscope for Tomorrow* on community cable television in Fairfax, Virginia, an experience that qualified her as an "agent provocateur."

Finkelstein was a workshop director for the International Women's Writing Guild for 15 years, has a Ph.D. in English, and has taught Western culture, literature, symbolism, and writing at several universities in the South, Southwest, and Midwest. In her teaching career she assisted over 30 of her students in winning local, state, regional, and national writing competitions and in getting their work published. She is the co-founder of Sunweavers, Inc., a nonprofit organization that assists writers, artists, and creative visionaries in getting their work out to the public.

Finkelstein is the author of two other books of poetry, *I Am Anima* and *Syzygy*; the metaphysical novel *Magicians*; and with Susan Smily has co-authored four other novels: three cozy mysteries in the Ariel Quigley series and the thriller *Walk-In*. She also assisted Smily in the realization of Powell Smily's 1970s novel, *Cross Currents*.

The Chef Who Died Sautéing won the Love Is Murder Readers' Choice Award (the Lovey) for Best First Novel, and was nominated for an Agatha Award that same year. *Walk-In* was a winner in the published fiction division of the Public Safety Writers Association competition, 2012.

To the embarrassment of some of her more traditional friends and academic colleagues, Finkelstein also does past-life and Tarot readings and occasionally talks to ghosts.

Other Books by the Author

Visit www.honorafinkelstein.com

Poetry:

I AM ANIMA: Songs of Yin Energy
Honora Finkelstein
El Amarna Publishing, July, 2012

KUNDALINI RISING: Songs of Power and Spirit
Honora Finkelstein
El Amarna Publishing, July, 2012

SYZYGY: Songs for Fools and Magicians
Honora Finkelstein
El Amarna Publishing, July, 2012

Available on Amazon as Paperbacks and eBooks

* * *

Magicians:
A Novel of Transformation and Co-Creation
Honora Finkelstein
El Amarna Publishing, October, 2011
Available on Amazon as a Paperback and eBook

* * *

The Ariel Quigley Mystery Series
(www.arielquigleymysteries.com)
by Honora Finkelstein and Susan Smily

The Chef Who Died Sautéing & A Killer Cookbook #1:
Recipes to Accompany "The Chef Who Died Sautéing"

The Lawyer Who Died Trying & A Killer Cookbook #2:
Recipes to Accompany "The Lawyer Who Died Trying"

The Reporter Who Died Probing & A Killer Cookbook #3:
Holiday Recipes to Accompany "The Reporter Who Died Probing"

Available on Amazon as Paperbacks and eBooks
Second Editions, El Amarna Publishing, April, 2012
Visit www.elamarnapublishing.com to learn more.

* * *

Cross-Currents
A Neo-Noir by Powell Smily
realized by Susan Smily and Honora Finkelstein
El Amarna Publishing, April, 2012
Available on Amazon as a Paperback and eBook

* * *

Walk-In
A Thriller by Honora Finkelstein and Susan Smily
Oak Tree Press, February, 2012
Available on Amazon as a Paperback and eBook

About El Amarna Publishing

El Amarna Publishing is dedicated to producing books, monographs, and e-books for an eclectic but discerning reading audience who enjoy the pursuit of leading edge ideas and philosophies.

We appreciate quality fiction and nonfiction of all genres. For example, we will consider publishing books on history or historical fiction; true detective stories or mysteries; science or science fiction; works on the American West or western novels; true ghost stories or paranormal fiction; women's literature or unique romantic fiction; and any other types of literature as long as the ideas presented are forward thinking and the writing is high quality.

We also plan to publish works of humor; unusual cookbooks; volumes on art, dance, drama, music, and poetry, as well as on the artists who create these things. We will promote well-researched approaches to mythology, symbolism, dreams, esoteric astrology, and divining, as well as metaphysics, mysticism, and magic; and we value the work of creative visionaries in all fields, especially in the categories of comparative religion, interfaith spirituality, personal growth, cultural history, humanistic psychology, and futurism.

Please visit our website for submission requirements: www.ElAmarnaPublishing.com.

www.ingramcontent.com/pod-product-compliance
Lightning Source LLC
Chambersburg PA
CBHW020444030426
42337CB00014B/1393